MW00513026

The Complete Air Fryer Cookbook 2021

Easy and Tasty Recipes for Beginners and Advanced to Lose Weight in Health

Ursula Mayert

Table of Contents

—

© Copyright 2020 by Ursula Mayert

The information in the following pages is broadly considered a truthful and accurate account of facts and as such, any inattention, use, or misuse of the information in question by the reader will render any resulting actions solely under their purview. There are no scenarios in which the publisher or the original author of this work can be in any fashion deemed liable for any hardship or damages that may befall them after undertaking information described herein.

Additionally, the information in the following pages is intended only for informational purposes and should thus be thought of as universal. As befitting its nature, it is presented without assurance regarding its prolonged validity or interim quality. Trademarks that are mentioned are done without written consent and can in no way be considered an endorsement from the trademark holder.

Introduction

An air fryer is a relatively new kitchen appliance that has proven to be very popular among consumers. While there are many different varieties available, most air fryers share many common features. They all have heating elements that circulate hot air to cook the food. Most come with pre-programmed settings that assist users in preparing a wide variety of foods.

Air frying is a healthier style of cooking because it uses less oil than traditional deep frying methods. While it preserves the flavor and quality of the food, it reduces the amount of fat used in cooking. Air frying is a common method for "frying" foods that are primarily made with eggs and flour. These foods can be soft or crunchy to your preference by using this method.

How air fryers work

Air fryers use a blower to circulate hot air around food. The hot air heats the moisture on the food until it evaporates and creates steam. As steam builds up around the food, it creates pressure that pulls moisture from the surface of the food and pushes it away from the center, forming small bubbles. The bubbles creates a layer of air that surrounds the food and creates a crispy crust.

Choosing an air fryer

When choosing an air fryer, look for one that has good reviews for customer satisfaction. Start with the features you need, such as power, capacity size and accessories. Look for one that is easy to use. Some air fryers on the market have a built-in timer and adjustable temperature. Look for one with a funnel to catch grease, a basket that is dishwasher-safe and parts that are easy to clean.

How To Use An Air Fryer

For best results, preheat the air fryer at 400 F for 10 minutes. Preheating the air fryer allows it to reach the right temperature faster. In addition, preheating the air fryer is essential to ensure that your food won't burn.

How to cook stuff in an Air Fryer

If you don't have an air fryer yet, you can start playing with your ovens by throwing some frozen fries in there and cooking them until they are browned evenly. Depending on your oven, take a look at the temperature. You may need to increase or decrease the time.

What Foods Can You Cook In An Air Fryer?

Eggs: While you can cook eggs in an air fryer, we don't recommend it because you can't control the cooking time and temperature as precisely as with a traditional frying pan or skillet. It's much easier to get unevenly cooked eggs. You also can't toss in any sauces or seasonings and you won't get crispy, golden brown edges.

Frozen foods: Generally, frozen foods are best cooked in the conventional oven because they need to reach a certain temperature to be properly cooked. The air fryer is not capable of reaching temperatures that result in food being fully cooked.

Dehydrated Foods: Dehydrated foods require deep-frying, which is not something you can do with an air fryer. When it comes to cooking dehydrated foods, the air fryer is not the best option.

Vegetables: You can cook vegetables in an air fryer but you have to make sure that the air fryer is not set at a temperature that will burn them.

To ensure that your vegetables aren't overcooked, start the air fryer with the basket off, then toss in the veggies once the air has heated up and there are no more cold spots.

Make sure to stir the vegetables every few minutes. Cooking them in the basket is also an option, but they may stick together a little bit.

Fries: Frying fries in an air fryer is a good way to get crispy, golden-brown fries without adding lots of oil. Compared to conventional frying, air frying yields fewer calories.

To cook french fries in an air fryer, use a basket or a rack and pour in enough oil to come about halfway up the height of the fries. For best results, make sure the fries are frozen. Turn the air fryer onto 400 degrees and set it for 12 minutes. If you want them extra crispy, you can set it for 18 minutes, but they may burn a bit.

Benefits of an air fryer:

• It's one of the easiest ways to cook healthy foods. Used 4-5 times a week, it's a healthier option than frying with oil in your conventional oven or using canned foods.

• Air fryer meals are an easy way to serve tasty food that doesn't take up lots of space. Air fryers make it possible to cook three times as much food as you can in your microwave.

• Air fryers have a small footprint and you can store them away in a cabinet when not in use.

•They are versatile kitchen appliances. You can use them to cook food for lunch, dinner and snacks.

• Air fryers require little to no fussing in the kitchen. You can use them with the lid on, which means there's less washing up to do.

Breakfast

Simple Cornbread

Preparation Time: 15 minutes

Cooking Time: 25 minutes

Servings: 8

Ingredients:

1. 1 cup cornmeal
2. ¾ cup all-purpose flour
3. 1 tablespoon sugar
4. 1½ teaspoons baking powder
5. ½ teaspoon baking soda
6. ¼ teaspoon salt

7. 1½ cups buttermilk

8. 6 tablespoons unsalted butter, melted

9. 2 large eggs, lightly beaten

Directions:

1. In a bowl, mix together the cornmeal, flour, sugar, baking soda, baking powder, and salt.

2. Take a separate bowl, mix well the buttermilk, butter, and eggs.

3. Then, add in the flour mixture and mix until just combined.

4. Set the temperature of Air Fryer to 360 degrees F. Lightly, grease an 8-inch baking dish.

5. Transfer the flour mixture evenly into the prepared baking dish.

6. Place the dish into an Air Fryer basket.

7. Air Fry for about 25 minutes or until a toothpick inserted in the center comes out clean, turning the dish once halfway through.

8. Remove from Air Fryer and place the dish onto a wire rack for about 10-15 minutes.

9. Carefully, take out the bread from dish and put onto a wire rack until it is completely cool before slicing.

10. Cut the bread into desired size slices and serve.

Nutrition:

Calories: 217

Carbohydrate: 24.9g

Protein: 5.6g
Fat: 10.9g
Sugar: 3.9g
Sodium: 286mg

Pineapple Cornbread

Preparation Time: 10 minutes

Cooking Time: 15 minutes

Servings: 5

Ingredients:

- 1 (8½-ounces) package Jiffy corn muffin
- 7 ounces canned crushed pineapple
- 1/3 cup canned pineapple juice
- 1 egg

Directions:

- In a bowl, mix together all the Ingredients.
- Set the temperature of Air Fryer to 330 degrees F. Grease a round cake pan. (6"x 3")
- Place the mixture evenly into the prepared pan.
- Arrange the cake pan into an Air Fryer basket.
- Air Fry for about 15 minutes or until a toothpick inserted in the center comes out clean.
- Remove from Air Fryer and place the pan onto a wire rack for about 10-15 minutes.
- Carefully, take out the bread from pan and put onto a wire rack until it is completely cool before slicing.
- Cut the bread into desired size slices and serve.

Nutrition:

Calories: 220

Carbohydrate: 40g

Protein: 3.8g

Fat: 6.4g

Sugar: 14.1g

Sodium: 423mg

Banana Oats

Preparation time: 5 minutes

Cooking time: 20 minutes

Servings: 4

Ingredients:

1. 2 cups old fashioned oats
2. 1/3 cup sugar
3. 1 teaspoon vanilla extract
4. 1 cup banana, peeled and mashed
5. 2 cups almond milk
6. 2 eggs, whisked
7. Cooking spray

Directions:

- In a bowl, combine the oats with the sugar and the other Ingredients except the cooking spray and whisk well.

- Heat up your air fryer at 340 degrees F, grease with cooking spray, add oats mix, toss, cover and cook for 20 minutes.
- Divide into bowls and serve for breakfast.

Nutrition:

Calories 260

Fat 4

Fiber 7

Carbs 9

Protein 10

Cheesy Bread And Eggs Bowls

Preparation time: 10 minutes

Cooking time: 30 minutes

Servings: 4

Ingredients:

1. 1 cup whole wheat bread, cubed

2. 1 cup mozzarella, shredded

3. 2 tablespoons olive oil

4. 1 red onion, chopped

5. 1 cup tomato sauce

6. Salt and black pepper to the taste

7. 8 eggs, whisked

Directions:

- Add the oil to your air fryer, heat it up at 340 degrees F, add onion, bread and the other Ingredients, toss, cook for 20 minutes shaking halfway.
- Divide between plates and serve for breakfast.

Nutrition:

Calories 211

Fat 8

Fiber 7

Carbs 14

Protein 3

Creamy Carrots Hash Mix

Preparation time: 10 minutes

Cooking time: 20 minutes

Servings: 4

Ingredients:

1. 1-pound carrots, peeled and cubed
2. 4 eggs, whisked
3. 1 cup coconut cream
4. 1 tablespoon olive oil
5. 1 red onion, chopped
6. 1 cup mozzarella, shredded
7. 1 tablespoon chives, chopped
8. Salt and black pepper to the taste

Directions:

- Heat up your air fryer with the oil at 350 degrees F, add the carrots hash and the other Ingredients, toss, cover, cook for 20 minutes, divide between plates and serve.

Nutrition:

Calories 231

Fat 9

Fiber 9

Carbs 8

Protein 12

Tomato Frittata

Preparation time: 10 minutes

Cooking time: 20 minutes

Servings: 4

Ingredients:

1. 1 cup cherry tomatoes, halved
2. 8 eggs, whisked
3. 1 red onion, chopped
4. 1 tablespoon olive oil
5. 1 tablespoon chives, chopped
6. ½ cup mozzarella, shredded
7. Salt and black pepper to the taste

Directions:

- In a bowl, combine the eggs with the tomatoes and the other Ingredients except the oil and whisk well,
- Heat up your air fryer at 300 degrees F, add the oil, heat it up, add the frittata mix, spread, and cook for 20 minutes.
- Divide between plates and serve.

Nutrition:

Calories 262

Fat 6

Fiber 9

Carbs 18

Protein 8

Strawberry Oatmeal

Preparation time: 4 minutes

Cooking time: 15 minutes

Servings: 4

Ingredients:

1. 1 cup old fashioned oats
2. ½ cup strawberries, chopped
3. 2 cups almond milk
4. 2 eggs, whisked
5. ¼ teaspoon vanilla extract

Directions:

-   In a bowl, combine the oats with the milk and the other Ingredients and whisk well.

- Heat up your air fryer at 350 degrees F, add berries mix, and cook for 15 minutes.
- Divide into bowls and serve for breakfast.

Nutrition:

Calories 180

Fat 5

Fiber 7

Carbs 12

Protein 5

Peppers and Tomato Eggs

Preparation time: 10 minutes

Cooking time: 20 minutes

Servings: 4

Ingredients:

1. 8 eggs, whisked
2. 1 cup roasted peppers, chopped
3. 1 cup tomatoes, chopped
4. Cooking spray
5. 1 tablespoon chives, chopped
6. ½ teaspoon sweet paprika
7. Salt and black pepper to the taste

Directions:

- In a bowl, combine the eggs with the peppers, tomatoes and the other Ingredients except the cooking spray and whisk well.
- Heat up your air fryer at 320 degrees F, grease with the cooking spray, add the eggs mix, cover and cook for 20 minutes.
- Divide between plates and serve for breakfast right away.

Nutrition:

Calories 190

Fat 7

Fiber 7

Carbs 12
Protein 4

Mushroom Oatmeal

Preparation time: 5 minutes

Cooking time: 20 minutes

Servings: 4

Ingredients:

1. 1 tablespoon avocado oil
2. 1 cup white mushrooms, sliced
3. 8 eggs, whisked
4. 1 cup old fashioned oats
5. 1 red onion, chopped
6. ½ cup heavy cream
7. Salt and black pepper to the taste
8. 1 tablespoon dill, chopped

Directions:

- In a bowl, mix the eggs with the oats, cream and the other Ingredients except the oil and the mushrooms and whisk.
- Heat up the air fryer with the oil at 330 degrees F, add the mushrooms and cook them for 5 minutes.
- Add the rest of the Ingredients, toss, and cook for 15 minutes more.
- Divide into bowls and serve for breakfast.

Nutrition:

Calories: 192

Fat: 6

Fiber: 6

Carbs: 14

Protein: 7

Cauliflower Hash

Preparation time: 10 minutes

Cooking time: 20 minutes

Servings: 4

Ingredients:

1. 1-pound cauliflower florets
2. 8 eggs, whisked
3. 1 red onion, chopped
4. A drizzle of olive oil
5. ½ teaspoon sweet paprika
6. ½ teaspoon coriander, ground
7. 1 cup mozzarella, shredded
8. Salt and black pepper to the taste

Directions:

1. Heat up the air fryer at 350 degrees F with a drizzle of oil, add the cauliflower, eggs and the other Ingredients, whisk and cook for 20 minutes.
2. Divide the hash between plates and serve for breakfast.

Nutrition:

Calories 194

Fat 4

Fiber 7

Carbs 11

Protein 6

Pesto Scramble

Preparation time: 3 minutes

Cooking time: 15 minutes

Servings: 4

Ingredients:

- 1 tablespoon butter, melted
- 8 eggs, whisked
- 1 tablespoon basil pesto
- ½ teaspoon sweet paprika
- 1 red onion, chopped
- Salt and black pepper to the taste
- 1 cup mozzarella cheese, grated

Directions:

- Heat up the air fryer at 350 degrees F with the butter, add the onion, eggs and the other Ingredients, whisk and cook for 15 minutes shaking the fryer halfway.
- Divide the scramble between plates and serve.

Nutrition:

Calories 187

Fat 6

Fiber 6

Carbs 13

Protein 5

Eggplant And Sausage Hash

Preparation time: 5 minutes

Cooking time: 20 minutes

Servings: 4

Ingredients:

1. 1 eggplant, cubed
2. 1 cup sausages, cubed
3. ½ pound hash browns
4. 2 eggs, whisked
5. ½ teaspoon turmeric powder
6. 1 tablespoon cilantro, chopped
7. 1 tablespoon olive oil
8. ½ cup mozzarella, shredded
9. Salt and black pepper to the taste

Directions:

- Heat up the air fryer with the oil at 360 degrees F, add the sausages and cook them for 5 minutes.
- Add the hash browns, eggplant and the other Ingredients, cover and cook for 15 minutes more.
- Divide everything between plates and serve.

Nutrition:

Calories 270

Fat 14

Fiber 3

Carbs 23

Protein 16

Salmon Eggs

Preparation time: 10 minutes

Cooking time: 15 minutes

Servings: 4

Ingredients:

1. 1 cup smoked salmon fillets, boneless and cubed
2. 8 eggs, whisked
3. 1 red onion, chopped
4. Cooking spray
5. ½ teaspoon sweet paprika
6. ½ teaspoon turmeric powder
7. ½ cup heavy cream
8. 1 tablespoon chives, chopped
9. Salt and black pepper to the taste

Directions:

- Set the air fryer at 380 degrees F and grease it with the cooking spray.
- In a bowl, mix the eggs with the salmon and the other Ingredients, whisk, pour into the fryer, cover and cook for 15 minutes.
- Divide between plates and serve for breakfast.

Nutrition:

Calories 170

Fat 2

Fiber 2

Carbs 12

Protein 4

Vanilla and Mango Bowls

Preparation Time: 5 minutes

Cooking Time: 10 minutes

Servings: 4

Ingredients:

1. 1 cup mango, peeled and cubed
2. 1 cup heavy cream
3. 2 tablespoons sugar
4. Juice of 1 lime
5. 2 teaspoons vanilla extract

Directions:

- In the air fryer's pan, combine the mango with the cream and the other Ingredients, cook at 370 degrees F for 10 minutes, divide into bowls and serve for breakfast.

Nutrition:

Calories 170

Fat 6

Fiber 5

Carbs 11

Protein 2

Chili Bowls

Preparation Time: 5 minutes

Cooking Time: 20 minutes

Servings: 4

Ingredients:

1. 1-pound beef stew meat, ground
2. 1 red onion, chopped
3. 1 teaspoon chili powder
4. 8 eggs, whisked
5. A drizzle of olive oil
6. ½ cup canned tomatoes, crushed
7. 1 red chili pepper, chopped
8. 2 tablespoons parsley, chopped
9. Salt and white pepper to the taste

Directions:

- Heat up the air fryer at 400 degrees F, grease with the oil, add the meat and the onion and cook for 5 minutes.
- Add the eggs and the other Ingredients, cover, cook for 15 minutes more, divide into bowls and serve for breakfast.

Nutrition:

Calories 200

Fat 6

Fiber 1

Carbs 11

Protein 3

Mushroom, Potato and Beef Bowls

Preparation Time: 5 minutes

Cooking Time: 20 minutes

Servings: 4

Ingredients:

1. 1-pound beef stew meat, ground
2. 1 tablespoon olive oil
3. ½ cup mushrooms, sliced
4. 1 cup gold potatoes, cubed
5. 1 red onion, chopped
6. 1 garlic clove, minced
7. ½ cup cherry tomatoes, halved
8. 4 eggs, whisked
9. Salt and black pepper to the taste

Directions:

- Heat up the air fryer with the oil at 400 degrees F, add the meat, mushrooms and onion and cook for 5 minutes.
- Add the potatoes and the other Ingredients, cook for 15 minutes more, divide between plates and serve for breakfast.

Nutrition:

Calories 160

Fat 2

Fiber 5

Carbs 12
Protein 9

Carrot Muffins

Preparation Time: 5 minutes

Cooking Time: 20 minutes

Servings: 4

Ingredients:

1. 3 eggs, whisked
2. 1 tablespoon butter, melted
3. 1 cup carrots, peeled and grated
4. 1 cup heavy cream
5. ½ cup almond flour
6. 1 cup almond milk
7. Cooking spray
8. 1 tablespoon baking powder

Directions:

- In a bowl, combine the eggs with the butter, carrots and the other Ingredients except the cooking spray, and whisk well.
- Grease a muffin pan that fits your air fryer with the cooking spray, divide the carrots mix inside, put the pan in the air fryer and cook at 392 degrees F for 20 minutes.
- Serve the muffins for breakfast.

Nutrition:

Calories 190

Fat 12

Fiber 2

Carbs 11

Protein 5

Breakfast Peppers Frittata

Preparation Time: 10 minutes

Cooking Time: 10 minutes

Servings: 2

Ingredients:

1. 2 large eggs
2. 1 tbsp bell peppers, chopped
3. 1 tbsp spring onions, chopped
4. 1 sausage patty, chopped
5. 1 tbsp butter, melted
6. 2 tbsp cheddar cheese
7. Pepper
8. Salt

Directions:

- Add sausage patty in air fryer baking dish and cook in air fryer 350 F for 5 minutes.
- Meanwhile, in a bowl whisk together eggs, pepper, and salt.
- Add bell peppers, onions and stir well.
- Pour egg mixture over sausage patty and stir well.
- Sprinkle with cheese and cook in the air fryer at 350 F for 5 minutes.
- Serve and enjoy.

Nutrition:

Calories 205

Fat 14.7g

Cholesterol 5g

Sugar 4g

Protein 12g

Cholesterol 221 mg

Scrambled Eggs

Preparation Time: 10 minutes

Cooking Time: 6 minutes

Servings: 2

Ingredients:

1. 4 eggs
2. 1/4 tsp garlic powder
3. 1/4 tsp onion powder
4. 1 tbsp parmesan cheese
5. Pepper
6. Salt

Directions:

- Whisk eggs with garlic powder, onion powder, parmesan cheese, pepper, and salt.

- Pour egg mixture into the air fryer baking dish.
- Place dish in the air fryer and cook at 360 F for 2 minutes. Stir quickly and cook for 3-4 minutes more.
- Stir well and serve.

Nutrition:

Calories 149

Fat 9.1g

Cholesterol 4.5g

Sugar 1.1g

Protein 11g

Cholesterol 325 mg

Sausage Egg Cups

Preparation Time: 10 minutes

Cooking Time: 10 minutes

Servings: 2

Ingredients:

1. 1/4 cup eggbeaters
2. 1/4 sausage, cooked and crumbled
3. 4 tsp jack cheese, shredded
4. 1/4 tsp garlic powder
5. 1/4 tsp onion powder
6. 4 tbsp spinach, chopped
7. Pepper
8. Salt

Directions:

- In a bowl, whisk together all Ingredientsuntil well combined.
- Pour batter into the silicone muffin molds and place in the air fryer basket.
- Cook at 330 F for 10 minutes.
- Serve and enjoy.

Nutrition:

Calories 90

Fat 5g

Cholesterol 1g

Sugar 0.2g

Protein 7g

Cholesterol 14 mg

Cheese Stuff Peppers

Preparation Time: 5 minutes

Cooking Time: 8 minutes

Servings: 8

Ingredients:

1. 8 small bell pepper, cut the top of peppers
2. oz. feta cheese, cubed
3. 1 tbsp. olive oil
4. 1 tsp Italian seasoning
5. 1 tbsp. parsley, chopped
6. ¼ tsp garlic powder
7. Pepper
8. Salt

Directions:

- In a bowl, toss cheese with oil and seasoning.
- Stuff cheese in each bell peppers and place into the air fryer basket.
- Cook at 400 F for 8 minutes.
- Serve and enjoy.

Nutrition:

Calories 88

Fat 5g

Cholesterol 9g

Sugar 6g

Protein 3g

Cholesterol 10 mg

Roasted Pepper Salad

Preparation Time: 10 minutes

Cooking Time: 10 minutes

Servings: 4

Ingredients:

1. 4 bell peppers
2. 2 oz. rocket leaves
3. 2 tbsp. olive oil
4. 4 tbsp. heavy cream
5. 1 lettuce head, torn
6. 1 tbsp. fresh lime juice
7. Pepper
8. Salt

Directions:

- Add bell peppers into the air fryer basket and cook for 10 minutes at 400 F.
- Remove peppers from air fryer and let it cool for 5 minutes.
- Peel cooked peppers and cut into strips and place into the large bowl.
- Add remaining Ingredients into the bowl and toss well.
- Serve and enjoy.

Nutrition:

Calories 160

Fat 13g

Cholesterol 11g

Sugar 6g

Protein 2g

Cholesterol 20 mg

Crust-Less Quiche

Preparation Time: 5 minutes

Cooking Time: 30 minutes

Servings: 2

Ingredients:

1. 4 eggs
2. ¼ cup onion, chopped
3. ½ cup tomatoes, chopped
4. ½ cup milk
5. 1 cup gouda cheese, shredded
6. Salt, to taste

Directions:

- Preheat the Air fryer to 340 o F and grease 2 ramekins lightly.
- Mix together all the ingredients in a ramekin until well combined.
- Place in the Air fryer and cook for about 30 minutes.
- Dish out and serve.

Nutrition:

Calories: 312

Fat: 15g

Saturated Fat: 4g

Trans Fat: 0g

Cholesterol: 14g

Fiber: 2g

Sodium: 403mg

Protein: 25g

Milky Scrambled Eggs

Preparation Time: 10 minutes

Cooking Time: 9 minutes

Servings: 2

Ingredients:

1. ¾ cup milk
2. 4 eggs
3. 8grape tomatoes, halved
4. ½ cup Parmesan cheese, grated
5. 1 tablespoon butter
6. Salt and black pepper, to taste

Directions:

- Preheat the Air fryer to 360 o F and grease an Air fryer pan with butter.

- Whisk together eggs with milk, salt and black pepper in a bowl.
- Transfer the egg mixture into the prepared pan and place in the Air fryer.
- Cook for about 6 minutes and stir in the grape tomatoes and cheese.
- Cook for about 3 minutes and serve warm.

Nutrition:

Calories: 312

Fat: 15g

Saturated Fat: 4g

Trans Fat: 0g

Cholesterol: 14g

Fiber: 2g

Sodium: 403mg

Protein: 25g

Toasties and Sausage In Egg Pond

Preparation Time: 10 minutes

Cooking Time: 22 minutes

Servings: 2

Ingredients:

1. 3 eggs
2. 2 cooked sausages, sliced
3. 1 bread slice, cut into sticks
4. 1/8 cup mozzarella cheese, grated
5. 1/8 cup Parmesan cheese, grated
6. ¼ cup cream

Directions:

- Preheat the Air fryer to 365 0 F and grease 2 ramekins lightly.
- Whisk together eggs with cream in a bowl and place in the ramekins.
- Stir in the bread and sausage slices in the egg mixture and top with cheese.
- Transfer the ramekins in the Air fryer basket and cook for about 22 minutes.
- Dish out and serve warm.

Nutrition:

Calories: 261

Fat: 15g

Saturated Fat: 4g

Trans Fat: 0g

Cholesterol: 14g

Fiber: 2g

Sodium: 403mg

Protein: 25g

Flavorful Bacon Cups

Preparation Time: 10 minutes

Cooking Time: 15 minutes

Servings: 6

Ingredients:

1. 6 bacon slices
2. 6 bread slices
3. 1 scallion, chopped
4. 3 tablespoons green bell pepper, seeded and chopped
5. 6 eggs
6. 2 tablespoons low-fat mayonnaise

Directions:

- Preheat the Air fryer to 375 0 F and grease 6 cups muffin tin with cooking spray.
- Place each bacon slice in a prepared muffin cup.
- Cut the bread slices with round cookie cutter and place over the bacon slices.
- Top with bell pepper, scallion and mayonnaise evenly and crack 1 egg in each muffin cup.
- Place in the Air fryer and cook for about 15 minutes.
- Dish out and serve warm.

Nutrition:

Calories: 260

Fat: 15g

Saturated Fat: 4g

Trans Fat: 0g

Cholesterol: 14g

Fiber: 2g

Sodium: 403mg

Protein: 25g

Crispy Potato Rosti

Preparation Time: 10 minutes

Cooking Time: 15 minutes

Servings: 2

Ingredients:

1. ½ pound russet potatoes, peeled and grated roughly
2. 1 tablespoon chives, chopped finely
3. 2 tablespoons shallots, minced
4. 1/8 cup cheddar cheese
5. ounces smoked salmon, cut into slices
6. 2 tablespoons sour cream
7. 1 tablespoon olive oil

8. Salt and black pepper, to taste

Directions:

- Preheat the Air fryer to 365 o F and grease a pizza pan with the olive oil.
- Mix together potatoes, shallots, chives, cheese, salt and black pepper in a large bowl until well combined.
- Transfer the potato mixture into the prepared pizza pan and place in the Air fryer basket.
- Cook for about 15 minutes and dish out in a platter.
- Cut the potato rosti into wedges and top with smoked salmon slices and sour cream to serve.

Nutrition:

Calories: 327

Fat: 15g

Saturated Fat: 4g

Trans Fat: 0g

Cholesterol: 14g

Fiber: 2g

Sodium: 403mg

Protein: 25g

Stylish Ham Omelet

Preparation Time: 10 minutes

Cooking Time: 30 minutes

Servings: 2

Ingredients:

1. 4 small tomatoes, chopped
2. 4 eggs
3. 2 ham slices
4. 1 onion, chopped
5. 2 tablespoons cheddar cheese
6. Salt and black pepper, to taste

Directions:

- Preheat the Air fryer to 390 o F and grease an Air fryer pan.
- Place the tomatoes in the Air fryer pan and cook for about 10 minutes.
- Heat a nonstick skillet on medium heat and add onion and ham.
- Stir fry for about 5 minutes and transfer into the Air fryer pan.
- Whisk together eggs, salt and black pepper in a bowl and pour in the Air fryer pan.
- Set the Air fryer to 335 o F and cook for about 15 minutes.
- Dish out and serve warm.

Nutrition:

Calories: 255

Fat: 15g

Saturated Fat: 4g

Trans Fat: 0g

Cholesterol: 14g

Fiber: 2g

Sodium: 403mg

Protein: 25g

Healthy Tofu Omelet

Preparation Time: 10 minutes

Cooking Time: 29 minutes

Servings: 2

Ingredients:

1. ¼ of onion, chopped
2. 12-ounce silken tofu, pressed and sliced
3. 3 eggs, beaten
4. 1 tablespoon chives, chopped
5. 1garlic clove, minced
6. 2 teaspoons olive oil
7. Salt and black pepper, to taste

Directions:

- Preheat the Air fryer to 355 0 F and grease an Air fryer pan with olive oil.
- Add onion and garlic to the greased pan and cook for about 4 minutes.
- Add tofu, mushrooms, chives, and season with salt and black pepper.
- Beat the eggs and pour over the tofu mixture.
- Cook for about 25 minutes, poking the eggs twice in between.
- Dish out and serve warm.

Nutrition:

Calories: 248

Fat: 29g

Saturated Fat: 3g

Trans Fat: 0g

Cholesterol: 31g

Fiber: 4g

Sodium: 374mg

Protein: 47g

Peanut Butter Banana Bread

Preparation Time: 15 minutes

Cooking Time: 40 minutes

Servings: 6

Ingredients:

1. 1 cup plus 1 tablespoon all-purpose flour
2. 1¼ teaspoons baking powder
3. 1 large egg
4. 2 medium ripe bananas, peeled and mashed
5. ¾ cup walnuts, roughly chopped
6. ¼ teaspoon salt, 1/3 cup granulated Sugar
7. ¼ cup canola oil, 2 tablespoons creamy peanut butter
8. 2 tablespoons sour cream, 1 teaspoon vanilla extract

Directions:

- Preheat the Air fryer to 330 o F and grease a non-stick baking dish. Mix together the flour, baking powder and salt in a bowl. Whisk together egg with Sugar, canola oil, sour cream, peanut butter and vanilla extract in a bowl. Stir in the bananas and beat until well combined. Now, add the flour mixture and fold in the walnuts gently.

- Mix until combined and transfer the mixture evenly into the prepared baking dish. Arrange the baking dish in an Air fryer basket and cook for about 40 minutes. Remove from the Air fryer and place onto a wire rack to cool. Cut the bread into desired size slices and serve.

Nutrition:

Calories: 510

Fat: 29g

Saturated Fat: 3g

Trans Fat: 0g

Cholesterol: 31g

Fiber: 4g

Sodium: 374mg

Protein: 47g

Yummy Savory French Toasts

Preparation Time: 10 minutes

Cooking Time: 4 minutes

Servings: 2

Ingredients:

1. ¼ cup chickpea flour
2. 3 tablespoons onion, chopped finely
3. 2 teaspoons green chili, seeded and chopped finely
4. Water, as required
5. 4 bread slices
6. ½ teaspoon red chili powder
7. ¼ teaspoon ground turmeric
8. ¼ teaspoon ground cumin

9. Salt, to taste

Directions:

- Preheat the Air fryer to 375 0 F and line an Air fryer pan with a foil paper.
- Mix together all the ingredients in a large bowl except the bread slices.
- Spread the mixture over both sides of the bread slices and transfer into the Air fryer pan.
- Cook for about 4 minutes and remove from the Air fryer to serve.

Nutrition:

Calories: 339

Fat: 12g

Saturated Fat: 2g

Trans Fat: 0g

Cholesterol: 16g

Fiber: 3.5g

Sodium: 362mg

Protein: 19g

Flaky Maple Donuts

Preparation Time: 10 minutes

Cooking Time: 15 minutes plus 1 hour to cool

Servings: 15

Ingredients:

1. 1 frozen puff pastry sheet (15 by 10 inches), thawed
2. 2 teaspoons all-purpose flour
3. 2½ cups powdered sugar
4. 3 tablespoons pure maple syrup
5. 2 tablespoons 2% milk
6. 2 tablespoons butter, melted
7. ½ teaspoon vanilla extract
8. ½ teaspoon ground cinnamon
9. Pinch salt

Directions:

- Put the puff pastry on a work surface dusted with the flour. Cut into 15 squares by cutting crosswise into five 3-inch-wide strips and then cutting each strip into thirds.
- Set or preheat the air fryer to 325°F. Put a parchment paper round in the bottom of the basket and add as many pastry squares as will fit without touching or overlapping.

- Bake for 14 to 19 minutes or until the donuts are browned and not doughy inside. Cool on a wire rack. Repeat with the remaining dough.
- In a small bowl, combine the powdered sugar, maple syrup, milk, melted butter, vanilla, cinnamon, and salt and mix with a wire whisk until combined.
- Let the donuts cool for about 1 hour, and then dip the top half of each in the glaze. Turn the donut over, glaze-side up, and put on wire racks. Let stand until set, then serve.

Nutrition:

Calories: 109

Total fat: 3g

Saturated fat: 1g

Cholesterol: 4mg

Sodium: 32mg

Carbohydrates: 21g

Fiber: 0g

Protein: 0g

Coffee cake Muffins

Preparation Time: 20 minutes

Cooking Time: 15 minutes

Servings: 6

Ingredients:

1. 1⅓ cups all-purpose flour, divided
2. 5 tablespoons butter, melted, divided
3. ¼ cup packed light brown sugar
4. ½ teaspoon ground cinnamon
5. ⅓ cup granulated sugar
6. ¼ cup 2% milk
7. 1 large egg
8. 1 teaspoon vanilla extract
9. 1 teaspoon baking powder
10. Pinch salt
11. Nonstick baking spray (containing flour)

Directions:

- In a small bowl, combine ⅓ cup of flour, 2½ tablespoons of butter, the brown sugar, and cinnamon and mix until crumbly. Set the streusel topping aside.
- In a medium bowl, combine the remaining 2½ tablespoons of butter, the granulated sugar, milk, egg, and vanilla and mix well.
- Add the remaining 1 cup flour, baking powder, and salt and mix just until combined.

- Spray 6 silicone muffin cups with baking spray.
- Spoon half of the batter into the prepared muffin cups. Top each with about 1 teaspoon of the streusel, then add the remaining batter. Sprinkle each muffin with the remaining streusel and gently press into the batter.
- Set or preheat the air fryer to 330°F. Place the muffin cups in the air fryer basket. Bake the muffins for 14 to 18 minutes or until a toothpick inserted into the center of a muffin comes out clean. Cool on a wire rack for 10 minutes, then remove the muffins from the silicone cups. Serve warm or cold.

Nutrition:

Calories: 285

Total fat: 11g

Saturated fat: 7g

Cholesterol: 57mg

Sodium: 122mg

Carbohydrates: 42g

Fiber: 1g

Protein: 4g

Baked Oatmeal Apple Cups

Preparation Time: 15 minutes

Cooking Time: 15 minutes

Servings: 6

Ingredients:

1. ½ cup unsweetened applesauce
2. 1 large egg
3. ⅓ cup packed light brown sugar
4. 2 tablespoons butter, melted
5. ½ cup 2% milk
6. 1⅓ cups old-fashioned rolled oats
7. 1 teaspoon ground cinnamon
8. ½ teaspoon baking powder
9. Pinch salt
10. ½ cup diced peeled apple

11. Nonstick baking spray (containing flour)

Directions:

- In a medium bowl, combine the applesauce, egg, brown sugar, melted butter, and milk and mix until combined.
- Add the oats, cinnamon, baking powder, and salt and stir until mixed. Stir in the apple.
- Spray 6 silicone muffin cups with baking spray. Divide the batter among the muffin cups.
- Set or preheat the air fryer to 350°F. Place the muffin cups in the air fryer basket. Bake the cups for 13 to 18 minutes or until they are set to the touch. Let cool for 15 minutes before serving.

Nutrition:

Calories: 254

Total fat: 8g

Saturated fat: 3g

Cholesterol: 43mg

Sodium: 82mg

Carbohydrates: 40g

Fiber: 4g

Protein: 8g

Bacon-Roasted Fruit with Yogurt

Preparation Time: 15 minutes

Cooking Time: 20 minutes

Servings: 4

Ingredients:

1. 3 bacon slices
2. 1 Granny Smith apple, peeled and cubed
3. 1 Bosc pear, peeled and cubed
4. 1 cup canned cubed pineapple
5. 2 tablespoons sugar
6. ½ teaspoon ground cinnamon
7. 2 cups plain Greek yogurt

Directions:

- Put a rack inside a 7-inch cake pan. Cut the bacon slices in half crosswise and put them on the rack.
- Set or preheat the air fryer to 350°F. Place the cake pan in the air fryer basket. Cook the bacon for 7 minutes, then check for doneness. Cook for another 2 to 3 minutes, if necessary, until crisp.
- Remove the bacon from the rack and place on paper towels to drain. Remove the rack and scoop all but 2 teaspoons of bacon fat out of the pan.
- Set or preheat the air fryer to 380°F. Add the apple, pear, and pineapple to the fat in the pan. Sprinkle with the sugar and cinnamon and toss.

- Roast the fruit for 10 to 15 minutes, stirring the mixture every 5 minutes, until the fruit is tender and browned around the edges.
- Crumble the bacon and add it to the fruit; serve over the yogurt.

Nutrition:

Calories: 211

Total fat: 7g

Saturated fat: 4g

Cholesterol: 24mg

Sodium: 203mg

Carbohydrates: 30g

Fiber: 3g

Protein: 8g

Scrambled Eggs with Cheese

Preparation Time: 5 minutes

Cooking Time: 14 minutes

Servings: 4

Ingredients:

1. 8 large eggs
2. ¼ cup sour cream
3. ¼ cup whole milk
4. ¼ teaspoon salt
5. Pinch freshly ground black pepper
6. 3 tablespoons butter, divided
7. 1 cup shredded Cheddar cheese
8. 1 tablespoon minced fresh chives

Directions:

- In a medium bowl, beat the eggs with the sour cream, milk, salt, and pepper until foamy.
- Put 2 tablespoons of butter in a cake barrel, put it in the air fryer, and set or preheat to 350°F. The butter will melt while the air fryer preheats.
- Remove the barrel from the air fryer basket. Add the egg mixture to the cake barrel and return to the air fryer.
- Cook for 4 minutes, then stir the eggs with a heatproof spatula.
- Cook for 3 minutes more minutes, then stir again.

- Cook for 3 minutes more minutes, then add the remaining 1 tablespoon of butter and the Cheddar and stir gently.
- Cook for 2 to 4 more minutes or until the eggs are just set.
- Remove the cake barrel from the air fryer and put the eggs in a serving bowl. Sprinkle with the chives and serve.

Nutrition:

Calories: 371;

Total fat: 31g;

Saturated fat: 16g;

Cholesterol: 433mg;

Sodium: 551mg;

Carbohydrates: 2g;

Fiber: 0g;

Protein: 20g

Soda Bread Currant Muffins

Preparation Time: 15 minutes

Cooking Time: 15 minutes

Servings: 6

Ingredients:

1. 1 cup all-purpose flour
2. 2 tablespoons whole wheat flour
3. 1 teaspoon baking powder
4. ⅛ teaspoon baking soda
5. Pinch salt
6. 3 tablespoons light brown sugar
7. ½ cup dried currants
8. 1 large egg

9. ⅓ cup buttermilk

10. 3 tablespoons butter, melted

11. Nonstick baking spray (containing flour)

Directions:

- In a medium bowl, combine the flours, baking powder, baking soda, salt, and brown sugar and mix until combined. Stir in the currants.
- In a small bowl, combine the egg, buttermilk, and melted butter and stir until blended.
- Add the egg mixture to the flour mixture and stir just until combined.
- Spray 6 silicone muffin cups with baking spray. Divide the batter among the muffin cups, filling each about two-thirds full.
- Set or preheat the air fryer 350°F. Set the muffin cups in the air fryer basket. Bake the muffins for 14 to 18 minutes or until a toothpick inserted in the center comes out clean.
- Cool on a wire rack for 10 minutes before serving.

Nutrition:

Calories: 204

Total fat: 7g

Saturated fat: 4g

Cholesterol: 47mg

Sodium: 140mg

Carbohydrates: 32g

Fiber: 2g

Protein: 5g

Raspberry-Stuffed French toast

Preparation Time: 15 minutes

Cooking Time: 8 minutes

Servings: 4

Ingredients:

1. 4 (1-inch-thick) slices French bread
2. 2 tablespoons raspberry jam
3. ⅓ cup fresh raspberries
4. 2 egg yolks
5. ⅓ cup 2% milk
6. 1 tablespoon sugar
7. ½ teaspoon vanilla extract
8. 3 tablespoons sour cream

Directions:

1. Cut a pocket into the side of each bread slice, making sure you don't cut through to the other side.
2. In a small bowl, combine the raspberry jam and raspberries and crush the raspberries into the jam with a fork.
3. In a shallow bowl, beat the egg yolks with the milk, sugar, and vanilla until combined.
4. Spread some of the sour cream in the pocket you cut in the bread slices, then add the raspberry mixture. Squeeze the edges of the bread slightly to close the opening.

5. Dip the bread in the egg mixture, letting the bread stand in the egg for 3 minutes. Flip the bread over and let stand on the other side for 3 minutes.
6. Set or preheat the air fryer to 375°F. Arrange the stuffed bread in the air fryer basket in a single layer.
7. Air fry for 5 minutes, then carefully flip the bread slices and cook for another 3 to 6 minutes, until the French toast is golden brown.

Nutrition:

Calories: 278

Total fat: 6g

Saturated fat: 3g

Cholesterol: 99mg

Sodium: 406mg

Carbohydrates: 46g

Fiber: 2g

Protein: 9g

Apple Roll-Ups

Preparation Time: 20 minutes

Cooking Time: 20 minutes

Servings: 8

Ingredients:

- 3 tablespoons ground cinnamon
- 3 tablespoons granulated sugar
- 2 teaspoons ground nutmeg
- 1 teaspoon ground cardamom
- ½ teaspoon ground allspice
- 2 large Granny Smith apples, peeled and cored
- 10 tablespoons butter, melted, divided
- 2 tablespoons light brown sugar
- 8 thin slices white sandwich bread, crusts cut off.

Directions:

1. In a 7-inch springform pan that has been wrapped in foil to prevent leaks, combine the olive oil, cherry tomatoes, plum tomatoes, tomato sauce, scallions, garlic, honey, salt, and cayenne.

2. Set or preheat the air fryer to 375°F. Set the pan in the air fryer basket. Cook the tomato mixture for 15 to 20 minutes, stirring twice during the cooking time, until the tomatoes are soft.

3. Use a fork to mash some of the tomatoes right in the pan, then stir the mashed tomatoes into the sauce.

4. Break the eggs into the sauce. Return the pan to the air fryer.

5. Cook for about 2 minutes or until the egg whites start to set. Remove the pan from the air fryer and gently stir the eggs into the sauce, marbling them through the sauce. Don't mix them in completely.

6. Continue cooking the mixture until the eggs are just set, 4 to 8 minutes more.

7. Cool for 10 minutes, then serve.

Nutrition:

Calories: 232

Total fat: 15g

 Saturated fat: 9g

Cholesterol: 38mg

Sodium: 249mg

Carbohydrates: 21g

Fiber: 4g

Protein: 4g

Pepper Egg Bites

Preparation Time: 15 minutes

Cooking Time: 15 minutes

Servings: 7

Ingredients:

- 5 large eggs, beaten
- 3 tablespoons 2% milk
- ½ teaspoon dried marjoram
- ⅛ teaspoon salt
- Pinch freshly ground black pepper
- ⅓ cup minced bell pepper, any color

- 3 tablespoons minced scallions
- ½ cup shredded Colby or Muenster cheese

Directions:

1. In a medium bowl, combine the eggs, milk, marjoram, salt, and black pepper; mix until combined.
2. Stir in the bell peppers, scallions, and cheese. Fill the 7 egg bite cups with the egg mixture, making sure you get some of the solids in each cup. Set or preheat the air fryer to 325°F.
3. Make a foil sling: Fold an 18-inch-long piece of heavy-duty aluminum foil lengthwise into thirds. Put the egg bite pan on this sling and lower it into the air fryer.
4. Leave the foil in the air fryer, but bend down the edges so they fit in the appliance.
5. Bake the egg bites for 10 to 15 minutes or until a toothpick inserted into the center comes out clean.
6. Use the foil sling to remove the egg bite pan. Let cool for 5 minutes, then invert the pan onto a plate to remove the egg bites. Serve warm.

Nutrition:

Calories: 87

Total fat: 6g

Saturated fat: 3g

Cholesterol: 141mg

Sodium: 149mg

Carbohydrates: 1g

Fiber: 0g

Protein: 7g

Crunchy Nut Granola

Preparation Time: 10 minutes

Cooking Time: 15 minutes

Servings: 6

Ingredients:

- 2 cups old-fashioned rolled oats
- ¼ cup pistachios
- ¼ cup chopped pecans
- ¼ cup chopped cashews
- ¼ cup honey
- 2 tablespoons light brown sugar
- 3 tablespoons butter
- ½ teaspoon ground cinnamon
- Nonstick baking spray (containing flour)
- ½ cup dried cherries

Directions:

1. In a medium bowl, combine the oats, pistachios, pecans, and cashews and toss.

2. In a small saucepan, combine the honey, brown sugar, butter, and cinnamon. Cook over low heat, stirring frequently, until the butter melts and the mixture is smooth, about 4 minutes. Pour over the oat mixture and stir.

3. Spray a 7-inch springform pan with baking spray. Add the granola mixture.

4. Set or preheat the air fryer to 325°F. Set the pan in the air fryer basket. Cook for 7 minutes, then remove the pan and stir. Continue cooking for 6 to 9 minutes or until the granola is light golden brown. Stir in the dried cherries.

5. Remove the pan from the air fryer and let cool, stirring a couple of times as the granola cools. Store in a covered container at room temperature up to 4 days.

Nutrition:

Calories: 446

Total fat: 18g

Saturated fat: 5g

Cholesterol: 15mg

Sodium: 51mg

Carbohydrates: 64g

Fiber: 7g

 Protein: 11g

Breakfast Pizza

Preparation Time: 10 minutes

Cooking Time: 15 minutes

Servings: 4

Ingredients:

- 4 (½-inch-thick) slices French bread, cut on a diagonal
- 6 teaspoons butter, divided
- 4 large eggs
- 2 tablespoons light cream
- ½ teaspoon dried basil
- ¼ teaspoon sea salt
- ⅛ teaspoon freshly ground black pepper
- 4 bacon slices, cooked until crisp and crumbled
- ⅔ cup shredded Colby or Muenster cheese

Directions:

1. Spread each slice of bread with 1 teaspoon of butter and place in the air fryer basket.
2. Set or preheat the air fryer to 350°F. Toast the bread for 2 to 3 minutes or until it's light golden brown. Remove from the air fryer and set aside on a wire rack.
3. Melt the remaining 2 teaspoons of butter in a 6-inch cake pan in the air fryer for 1 minute. Remove the basket from the air fryer.
4. In a medium bowl, beat together the eggs, cream, basil, salt, and pepper and add to the melted butter in the pan. Return the basket to the air fryer. Cook for 3 minutes, then stir. Cook for another 3 to 5 minutes or until the eggs are just set. Remove the eggs from the pan and put them in a bowl.
5. Top the bread with the scrambled eggs mixture, bacon, and cheese. Put back in the air fryer basket. Cook for 4 to 8 minutes or until the cheese is melted and starting to turn brown in spots.
6. Let cool for 5 minutes and serve.

Nutrition:

Calories: 425

Total fat: 23g

Saturated fat: 11g

Cholesterol: 233mg

Sodium: 947mg

Carbohydrates: 34g

Fiber: 1g
Protein: 21g

Veggie Frittata

Preparation Time: 15 minutes

Cooking Time: 25 minutes

Servings: 4

Ingredients:

- ¼ cup chopped red bell pepper
- ¼ cup chopped yellow summer squash
- 2 tablespoons chopped scallion
- 2 tablespoons butter
- 5 large eggs, beaten

- ¼ teaspoon sea salt
- ⅛ teaspoon freshly ground black pepper
- 1 cup shredded Cheddar cheese, divided

Directions:

1. In a 7-inch cake pan, combine the bell pepper, summer squash, and scallion. Add the butter.
2. Set or preheat the air fryer to 350°F. Set the cake pan in the air fryer basket. Cook the vegetables for 3 to 4 minutes or until they are crisp-tender. Remove the pan from the air fryer.
3. In a medium bowl, beat the eggs with the salt and pepper. Stir in half of the Cheddar. Pour into the pan with the vegetables.
4. Return the pan to the air fryer and cook for 10 to 15 minutes, then top the frittata with the remaining cheese. Cook for another 4 to 5 minutes or until the cheese is melted and the frittata is set. Cut into wedges to serve.

Nutrition:

Calories: 260

Total fat: 21g

Saturated fat: 11g

Cholesterol: 277mg

Sodium: 463mg

Carbohydrates: 2g

Fiber: 0g

Protein: 15g

Spicy Hash Brown Potatoes

Preparation Time: 15 minutes

Cooking Time: 20 minutes

Servings: 4

Ingredients:

- 2 tablespoons chili powder
- 2 teaspoons ground cumin
- 2 teaspoons smoked paprika
- 1 teaspoon garlic powder
- 1 teaspoon cayenne pepper
- 1 teaspoon freshly ground black pepper
- 2 large russet potatoes, peeled
- 2 tablespoons olive oil
- ⅓ cup chopped onion
- 3 garlic cloves, minced

- ½ teaspoon sea salt

Directions:

1. For the spice mix: In a small bowl, combine the chili powder, cumin, smoked paprika, garlic powder, cayenne, and black pepper. Transfer to a screw-top glass jar and store in a cool, dry place. (Some of the spice mix is used in this recipe; save the rest for other uses.)
2. Grate the potatoes in a food processor or on the large holes of a box grater. Put the potatoes in a bowl filled with ice water, and let stand for 10 minutes.
3. When the potatoes have soaked, drain them, then dry them well with a kitchen towel.
4. Put the olive oil, onion, and garlic in a 7-inch cake pan.
5. Set or preheat the air fryer to 400°F. Put the onion mixture in the air fryer and cook for 3 minutes, then remove.
6. Put the grated potatoes in a medium bowl and sprinkle with 2 teaspoons of spice mixture and toss. Add to the cake pan with the onion mixture.
7. Cook in the air fryer for 10 minutes, then stir the potatoes gently but thoroughly. Cook for 8 to 12 minutes more or until the potatoes are crisp and light golden brown. Season with salt.

Nutrition:

Calories: 235

Total fat: 8g

Saturated fat: 1g

Cholesterol: 0mg

Sodium: 419mg

Carbohydrates: 39g

Fiber: 5g

Protein: 5g

Sage and Pear Sausage Patties

Preparation Time: 15 minutes

Cooking Time: 20 minutes

Servings: 6

Ingredients:

- 1pound ground pork
- ¼ cup diced fresh pear
- 1 tablespoon minced fresh sage leaves
- 1 garlic clove, minced
- ½ teaspoon sea salt
- ⅛ teaspoon freshly ground black pepper

Directions:

1. In a medium bowl, combine the pork, pear, sage, garlic, salt, and pepper, and mix gently but thoroughly with your hands.
2. Form the mixture into 8 equal patties about ½ inch thick.
3. Set or preheat the air fryer to 375°F. Arrange the patties in the air fryer basket in a single layer. You may have to cook the patties in batches.
4. Cook the sausages for 15 to 20 minutes, flipping them halfway through the cooking time, until a meat thermometer registers 160°F. Remove from the air fryer, drain on paper towels for a few minutes, and then serve.

Nutrition:

Calories: 204

Total fat: 16g

Saturated fat: 6g

Cholesterol: 54mg

Sodium: 236mg

Carbohydrates: 1g

Fiber: 0g

Protein: 13g

Bacon Bombs

Preparation Time: 10 minutes

Cooking Time: 16 minutes

Servings: 4

Ingredients:

- 3 center-cut bacon slices
- 3 large eggs, lightly beaten
- 1 oz 1/3-less-fat cream cheese, softened
- 1 tbsp chopped fresh chives
- 4 oz fresh whole wheat pizza dough
- Cooking spray

Directions:

1. Sear the bacon slices in a skillet until brown and crispy then chop into fine crumbles. Add eggs to the same pan and cook for 1 minute then stir in cream cheese, chives and bacon. Mix well, then allow this egg filling to cool down. Spread the pizza dough and slice into four - 5inches circles. Divide the egg filling on top of each circle and seal its edge to make dumplings. Place the bacon bombs in the Air Fryer basket and spray them with cooking oil. Set the Air Fryer basket inside the Air Fryer toaster oven and close the lid. Select the Air Fry mode at 350 degrees F temperature for 6 minutes. Serve warm.

Nutrition:

Calories: 278
Protein: 7.9g
Carbs: 23g
Fat: 3.9g

Morning Potatoes

Preparation Time: 10 minutes

Cooking Time: 23 minutes

Servings: 4

Ingredients:

- 2 russet potatoes, washed & diced
- ½ tsp salt
- 1 tbsp. olive oil
- ¼ tsp garlic powder
- Chopped parsley, for garnish

Directions:

1. Soak the potatoes in cold water for 45 minutes, then drain and dry them. Toss potato cubes with garlic powder, salt, and olive oil in the Air Fryer basket. Set the Air Fryer basket inside the Air Fryer toaster oven and close the lid. Select the Air Fry mode at400 degrees F temperature for 23 minutes. Toss them well when cooked halfway through then continue cooking. Garnish with chopped parsley to serve.

Nutrition:

Calories: 146

Protein: 6.2g

Carbs: 41.2g

Fat: 5g

Breakfast Pockets

Preparation Time: 10 minutes

Cooking Time: 10 minutes

Servings: 6

Ingredients:

- 1 box puff pastry sheet
- 5 eggs
- ½ cup loose sausage, cooked
- ½ cup bacon, cooked
- ½ cup cheddar cheese, shredded

Directions:

1. Stir cook egg in a skillet for 1 minute then mix with sausages, cheddar cheese, and bacon. Spread the pastry sheet and cut it into four rectangles of equal size.

2. Divide the egg mixture over each rectangle. Fold the edges around the filling and seal them. Place the pockets in the Air Fryer basket. Set the Air Fryer basket inside the Air Fryer toaster oven and close the lid. Select the Air Fry mode at 370 degrees F temperature for 10 minutes. Serve warm.

Nutrition:

Calories: 387

Protein: 14.6g

Carbs: 37.4g

Fat: 6g

Avocado Flautas

Preparation Time: 10 minutes

Cooking Time: 24 minutes

Servings: 8

Ingredients:

- 1 tbsp butter
- 8 eggs, beaten
- ½ tsp salt
- ¼ tsp pepper
- 1 ½ tsp cumin
- 1 tsp chili powder
- 8 fajita-size tortillas
- 4 oz cream cheese, softened
- 8 slices cooked bacon
- Avocado Crème:
- 2 small avocados
- ½ cup sour cream
- 1 lime, juiced
- ½ tsp salt
- ¼ tsp pepper

Directions:

1. In a skillet, melt butter and stir in eggs, salt, cumin, pepper, and chili powder, then stir cook for 4 minutes. Spread all the tortillas and top them with cream cheese and bacon. Then divide the egg scramble on top and finally add cheese. Roll the tortillas to seal the filling inside. Place 4 rolls in the Air Fryer basket. Set the Air Fryer basket inside the Air Fryer toaster oven and close the lid. Select the Air Fry mode at 400 degrees F temperature for 12 minutes. Cook the remaining tortilla rolls in the same manner. Meanwhile, blend avocado crème ingredients in a blender then serves with warm flautas.

Nutrition:

Calories: 212

Protein: 17.3g

Carbs: 14.6g

Fat: 11.8g

Cheese Sandwiches

Preparation Time: 10 minutes

Cooking Time: 10 minutes

Servings: 2

Ingredients:

- 1 egg
- 3 tbsp half and half cream
- ¼ tsp vanilla extract
- 2 slices sourdough, white or multigrain bread
- 2½ oz sliced Swiss cheese

- 2 oz sliced deli ham
- 2 oz sliced deli turkey
- 1 tsp butter, melted
- Powdered sugar
- Raspberry jam, for serving

Directions:

1. Beat egg with half and half cream and vanilla extract in a bowl. Place one bread slice on the working surface and top it with ham and turkey slice and swiss cheese.
2. Place the other bread slice on top, then dip the sandwich in the egg mixture, then place it in a suitable baking tray lined with butter. Set the baking tray inside the Air Fryer toaster oven and close the lid. Select the Air Fry mode at 350 degrees F temperature for 10 minutes. Flip the sandwich and continue cooking for 8 minutes. Slice and serve.

Nutrition:

Calories: 412

Protein: 18.9g

Carbs: 43.8g

Fat: 24.8g

Conclusion

Thanks for making it to the end of this book. An air fryer is a relatively new addition to the kitchen, and it's easy to see why people are getting excited about using it. With an air fryer, you can make crispy fries, chicken wings, chicken breasts and steaks in minutes. There are many delicious foods that you can prepare without adding oil or grease to your meal. Again make sure to read the instructions on your air fryer and follow the rules for proper usage and maintenance. Once your air fryer is in good working condition, you can really get creative and start experimenting your way to healthy food that tastes great.

That's it! Thank you!

CPSIA information can be obtained
at www.ICGtesting.com
Printed in the USA
LVHW081044120521
687195LV00015B/366/J

9 781801 839730